Food For The UnPrepped

Frances Bryant

Published 2024 by Frances Bryant

Copyright Frances Bryant

ambrolen@gmail.com

Cover art-Shan Primrose

Illustrations- Shan Primrose, Frances Bryant.

Some illustrations created by AI

Photos- Frances Bryant

ISBN- 978-0-648826354

I would like to acknowledge the traditional owners of the land this book was produced on, the Kirrae Whurrong and Gunditjmara people, and their leaders past and present.

Food For The Unprepped

A guide to food sources in a crisis.

Written by

Frances Bryant

CONTENTS

Introduction

Book one -

Food For Survivors of the Zombie Apocalypse: An introduction to edible weeds.

Book two-

Unexpectdly Edible: Common garden plants you could eat (if you had to)

Conclusion

Introduction

Hypothetical:

It's happened. There is an unforeseen, unpredictable, worldwide crisis unfolding before your very eyes. Your life is in danger; you have no electricity, no communications, no expectations of any help coming any time soon.

You've heard, and read about, scenarios where these circumstances could occur; nuclear war, viral pandemics, zombie attack, even aliens attacking from Mars! But you, in your infinite wisdom, have decided these things are extremely unlikely to happen, let alone affect you, so you've left yourself unprepared., or as I like to say, unprepped. No way will you sink to the paranoid lows of those kooky 'preppers'! No digging bunkers, storing a year's worth of canned goods, or packing a 'bug out' bag for you! Well, now it's time to reap what your complacency has sown…

Reality:

Don't worry! The simple fact you have decided to buy this book is a good indication you have got your head screwed on right, and you will be able to utilise the information contained within to survive at least the first few weeks of whichever calamity comes first. At this point we would do well to have at least a little hope that help would indeed come, and that help would be of the beneficial kind which will protect and nurture us. Fingers crossed.

This book is a combination of two books I have written previously.

'Food For Survivors of the Zombie Apocalypse: An introduction to edible weeds' is, as the title states, an introduction to some of the plants generally considered to be weeds, which we can eat.

It is set against the backdrop of a Zombie Apocalypse and includes some survival tips related to that particular event, but those tips are easily transferable to any other crisis event. There are a few recipes given, and a few illustrations to aid in the correct identification of plants.

It would be of untold assistance to your survival if you were at least a little familiar with which weeds are commonly growing around your immediate area before any crisis, but there is also a very handy list of plants you SIMPLY MUST NOT EAT included in the text. I have added some weed species to the contents list, which extends the range of plants available to aid in your survival.

As I have no medical qualifications, I have not delved into the medicinal qualities of any plants, but further investigations on your own part could be a good idea.

'Unexpectedly Edible: Common garden plants you could eat (If you had to)' is the second part of this extended offering.

As the title suggests, the information included pertains to plants we grow as ornamental plants in our gardens, which can also be eaten. Many plants we grow have, in the past, been used as food sources in their native habitats, but this knowledge has disappeared over time as commercially grown food plants have become our main source of nutrition.

Learn which plants you might already have growing, or can easliy access, which could be valuable survival resources.

In 'normal' times, I would much prefer to grow many of these solely for their ornamental values, but if my life depended on it, I would most certainly chop up that Dahlia tuber to chuck in the soup pot!

Be safe, be a survivor.

Frances Bryant.

*Special note: The 'Z' on the collar of the dog on the covers is solely to indicate the dog's name is Zeus. There is no other reason. FB.

Book One

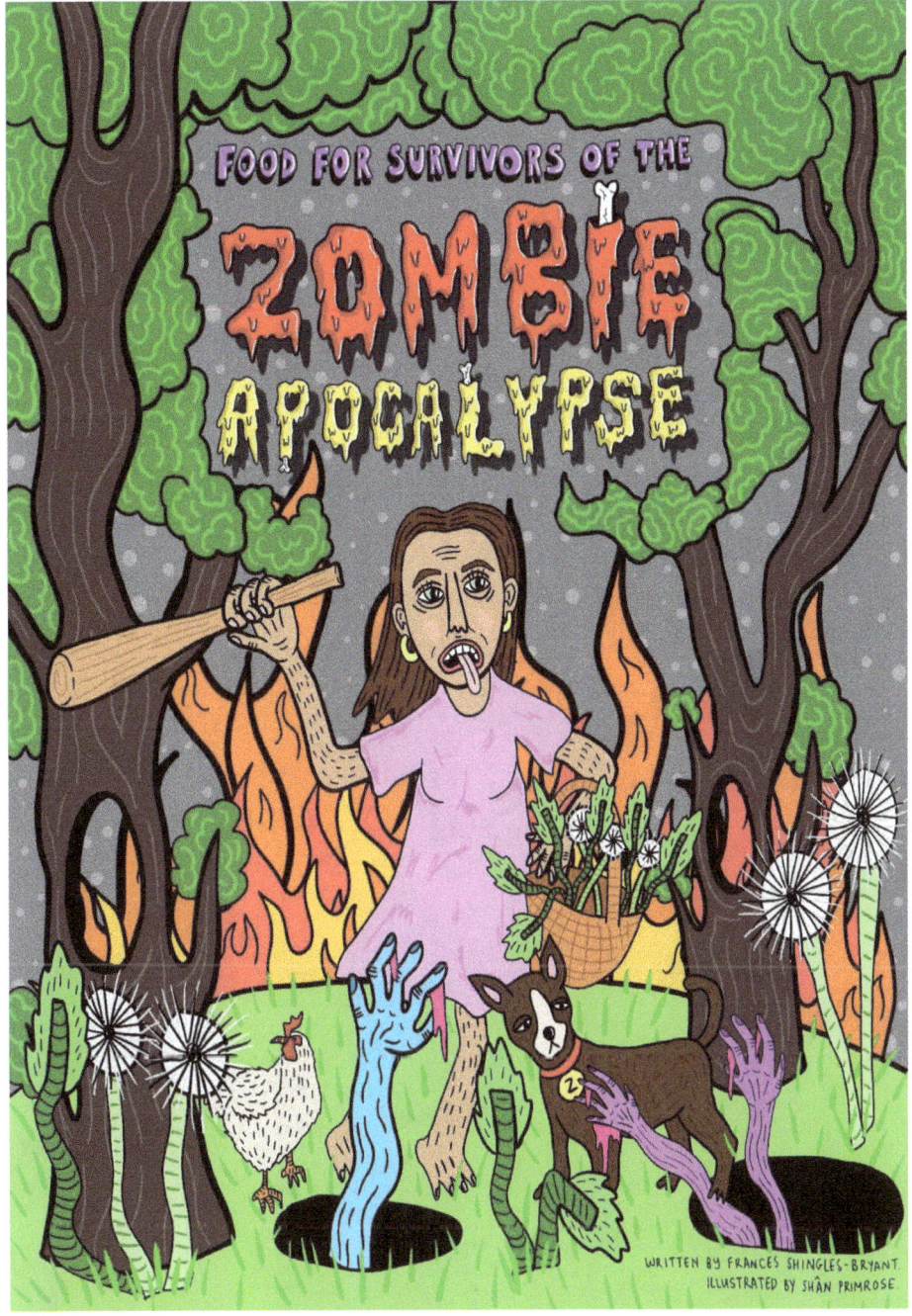

Produced by Frances Bryant

Copyright 2020

ISBN 9780648826316

ambrolen@gmail.com

Cover and good art work by

Shan Primrose (shanprimroseart.com)

Doodles for ID purposes by

Frances Bryant.

For the Survivors

Contents

- Chapter 1: Introduction

      (So, you've survived)

- Plant list

- Chapter 2: Plants formerly known as weeds suitable to eat in a post-zombie apocalypse world

      (Some recipes and information)

- Chapter 3: Tips and hints on surviving in a post-zombie apocalypse world

      (Thoughts and prayers)

- A few final words

shanprimroseart

Chapter 1: Introduction

So, you've survived the first days of the Zombie Apocalypse and you're adjusting to life in the new world. You've got your water source, you've got your security sorted, you've got your people.

The zombies want to eat brains, but you're not prepared to do the same thing!

What do you eat? and how can you safely forage for food while dodging zombies and marauding groups of other survivors? Don't kid yourself, it's going to be a dog eat dog world for some time yet! (Hopefully you don't have to eat Zeus, dogs will be valuable for security and protection, but be prepared to if needs be.)

Getting back to what you will eat.

With any luck you will be able to secure a safe place, if you haven't already, with the facilities to grow some vegetables and cook your food without threat of

Zombies smelling it (although I'm sure they're only attracted by noise and the scent of human brains if they get close enough)

This may not be enough though; it will depend on the number and types of people you have managed to bring together in these horrific times, the elderly and the very young could be problematic but they will need to be cared for or there's no point in the human race even surviving!

The human body requires many different nutrients to keep fit and healthy and be able to fend off Zombie attack, so having the knowledge to be able to supplement what you can grow with foods foraged from the outside will be invaluable.

Now, for most of our lives we have been conditioned to accept some plants as food, some as ornaments, and some as weedy pests that nobody wants in their lawn or on their paths and driveways. I have news for you! Those dandelions you've dug out of the lawn, and that Portulacayou've poisoned to make your driveway pristine, are your new pathway to surviving in a cold, dark, and dangerous world.

The plants discussed in this book, and more, are widely available and usually within easy reach of your heavily barricaded front door. This book will provide you with a few ideas to keep the vitamins, minerals and fibre sourced from these plants in your body to maintain fighting fitness and mental acuity; your ideas on what will be a suitable protein source is completely up to you...

Note: I'm hoping you have had the foresight to print out or buy this book as a handy reference to keep in your Apocalypse Pack, or, if you are frantically researching before internet access and electricity are lost to ordinary survivors like you forever, write down some of the recipes, and tips and hints in the following chapters NOW!

*If, by chance, you just happen to be reading this and there is no immediate danger of a zombie apocalypse, please be cautious if you want to actually try any of the following ideas and recipes. Tips and hints 6 is a good one to keep in mind.

Be safe. Be a survivor!

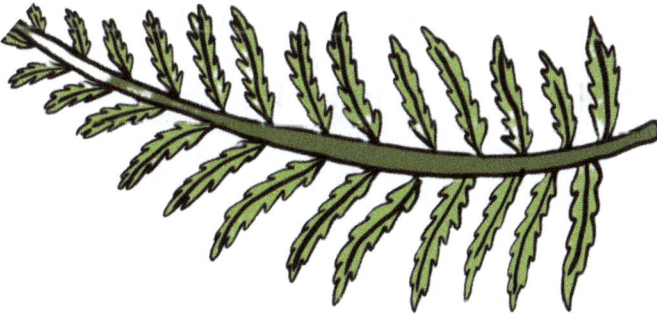

List of plants

Dandelion (Taraxacum officinale)

Catsear (Hypochaeris radicata)

Portulaca (Portulaca oleracea)

Stinging nettles (Urtica diocia)

Chickweed (Stellaria media)

Mallow (Malva neglecta)

Sticky weed (Galium aparine)

Goosefoot (Chenopodium album)

Ribwort Plantain (Plantago lanceolata)

Black Nightshade (Solanum nigra)

Flickweed (Cardamine hirsuta)

shanprimroseart

Chapter 2: Plants formerly known as weeds suitable to eat in a post-zombie apocalypse world

(some recipes and information)

<u>Dandelion (Taraxacum officinale)</u>

The leaves of the Dandelion plant can be a little bitter if they are older and/or not fresh. Young leaves can be eaten raw in salads and stir fries while older leaves can be dried and used as an herbal tea. The roots of the Dandelion have long been used as a coffee substitute which is caffeine free (recipe following). Although caffeine would be handy to give you an edge over a zombie, it is also a diuretic which can dehydrate your body.

The bright yellow flowers can be used raw in a salad but are delicious cooked as well, a tasty fried Dandelion flower recipe to follow. Dandelion flowers are high in vit A, Vit C and Lutein which is good for your eyes (handy!)

Dandelions are also a good blood purifier and builder.

Dig out a heap of dandelion roots (Remember you are going to be depleted of nutrition so it will take a lot of energy. If you are going to use dandelions as coffee over the year you will need a lot.) Wash, dry, and slice into 'chip' shaped pieces. Lay the chips out somewhere to dry. Chop them finer and roast them in whatever you have sourced for an oven.

Dandelion root Coffee:

Dig out a heap of dandelion roots (Remember you are going to be depleted of nutrition so it will take a lot of energy. If you are going to use dandelions as coffee over the year you will need a lot.) Wash, dry, and slice into 'chip' shaped pieces. Lay the chips out somewhere to dry. Chop them finer and roast them in whatever you have sourced as an oven.

Dandelion and Pumpkin kernel pesto:

Hopefully you've managed to secure a patch of earth in your compound to start a vegetable patch. One of the easiest things to grow in the warmer months with the least energy is a pumpkin vine. Using the seeds you don't keep for growing next season you can make a tasty mixture together with dandelion leaves which will add flavour to pretty much anything. Roast the pumpkin seeds then mash them together with garlic (another easy plant to grow) to taste; use the flat rock/round rock combo or a mortar and pestle. Chop steamed dandelion leaves into the mix and stir everything together, chopping and mixing until it forms a paste. A little oil will make this easier if you have any. Add a tiny sprinkle from your salt and pepper supply (see Tips and hints 2) for the extra taste.

Fried Dandelion flowers:

Pick whole flowers, dip them in batter made of flour (if you have any) and water and either shallow fry or deep fry (depending on your oil reserves). If you haven't managed to source or make flour you can shallow fry the flowers uncoated and perhaps grate or chop garlic and other herbs over the top.

Even though Dandelions are very common make sure you don't over harvest the flowers as they are required by the plant for reproduction which will keep supplies going (See Tips and Hints 1).

Dandelion roots:

the tap root can be boiled and eaten as for a carrot. Peel off the skin though, as it is bitter.

Grows: Best in Spring/Summer

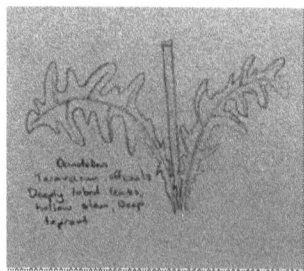

Catsear (Hypochaeris radicata)

Catsear is plant that looks incredibly like Dandelions, so much so one of its other names is False Dandelion. The flowers are very similar as are the leaves, one point of difference is the leaves of Catsear have fine hairs where Dandelions do not. Another difference is the stalk of Dandelions are hollow.

Visual differences aside, Catsear can be used in a very similar way to Dandelions except the taproot is much smaller; Dandelion chips are much more difficult so I probably wouldn't waste the energy on doing that.

Grows best: late spring/summer

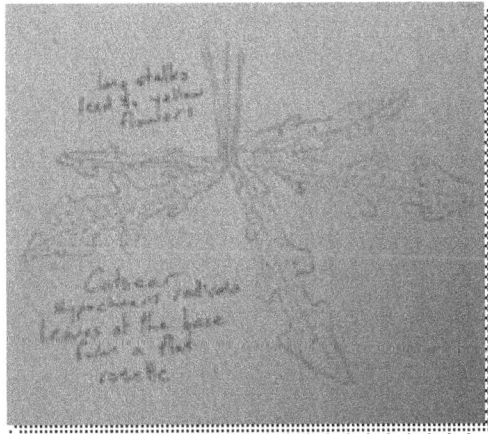

Portulaca (Portulaca oleracea)

Use the whole of the Portulaca plant in salads and anywhere else you would normally use a vegetable such as spinach. This plant is very high in omega 3 Fatty acids which is good for heart function; Omega 3 Fatty acids are usually known to be sourced from fish and flax seeds. Fish could be caught if you were lucky enough to be near a big enough water body, but flax seed production would be too problematic to be worth the effort. Portulaca also contains some oxalic acid so some care should be taken if you don't have much else available and need to eat a lot. Cooking can reduce the levels of Oxalic Acid, but overcooking will destroy much of the more beneficial components, so it's just another conundrum, risk poisoning? Or gain nutrients?

Portulaca can be eaten raw, steamed, fried, or any other way you can manage, it is particularly nice eaten with tomatoes (add tomatoes to your 'must grow' list)

Grows: spring/summer

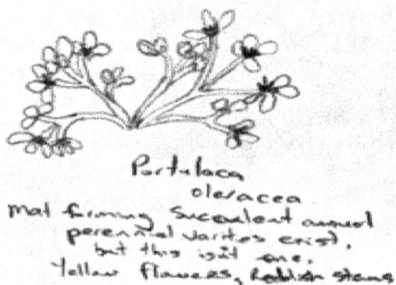

Portulaca
oleracea
Mat forming Succulent annual
perennial varities exist,
but this is it one.
Yellow flowers, Reddish stems

Stinging nettles (Urtica diocia)

Stinging nettles are a builder of good, strong blood as they are full of chlorophyll and iron. The leaves of Stinging Nettle can be used fresh in soups or dried as a tea which will last through the year. The stinging sensation you feel when you touch this plant with the bare hand is caused by irritating hairs which disappear once the plant is cooked in hot water. Use gloves to avoid this when harvesting. I am assuming the nettles will still irritate Zombies so keeping note of large patches could possibly be used as part of escape/attack plans; something to consider.

Nettle gnocchi: (assuming you have sourced or grown all the following ingredients. Of them al,l flour is one resource that will be difficult to source once supplies run out)

- Nettle leaves,
- potatoes,
- salt, pepper,
- flour,
- eggs.

Method: Cook the nettles and potatoes separatcly, mash the potatoes and add the nettles, and one or two eggs (see Tips and Hints 4). Next mix flour in to get a doughy consistency. Form into little balls and drop into boiling water until they float.

You'll probably have to boil the nettles thoroughly, so they break down better and blend in when mixed with the potatoes.

Nettle soup:

- Nettles,
- Stock (or plain water if you're not lucky enough to have found stock or made some)
- Potatoes
- Salt
- pepper

Method: Blanch the nettles in boiling water for five seconds before using, breaking down the stinging hairs, whilst Boiling some potatoes in stock of some description if you're lucky enough to have some, or just plain water.

Add the nettles and cook until soft. Add any other vegetables you have, including onion weed if it has appeared yet (see tips and hints 8). No electricity means no blending however, so it will be chunky but tasty and nutritious.

Grows: winter months

Chickweed (Stellaria media)

A plant high in protein and many other essential minerals, it is best eaten fresh to retain its nutrients. It can be used in salads, soups or stir-fries much as any other leafy green vegetable. It is also a great food for poultry

Chickweed can be used as a poultice for rashes and sores. Simply wash the plant and apply directly to closed wounds. It can be also be cooked and cooled, then placed under a wrapping to treat deeper wounds such as muscle tears (read more about medicinal plants in the companion booklet to this one: So You've been Injured, Which weeds can be substituted For Modern Medicine?)

Grows: late winter and spring

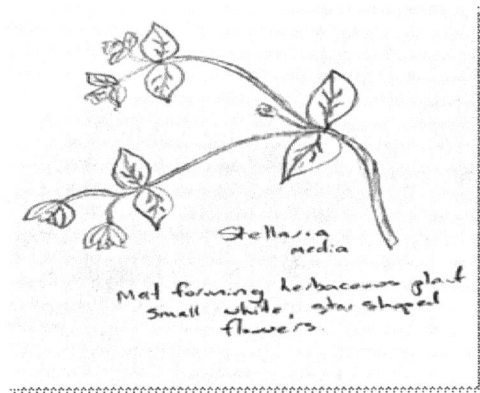

Stellaria media

Mat forming herbaceous plant
Small white, star shaped flowers.

Mallow (Malva neglecta)

All parts of Mallow can be eaten as a vegetable substitute. The leaves, roots and flowers are apparently quite tasteless so it will need to be eaten with something more flavoursome. It is very high in Vitamins A, B, and C, Calcium, Potassium, and Magnesium so it's a valuable plant to find. The seed heads can be eaten as well, they look a little like cheese rounds and can have a slightly nutty flavour. They can be pickled like a caper. Dried leaves can be used for a tea., the roots can be boiled, and the water beaten to make a meringue like egg substitute (once again, there will probably be no power so this could be time and energy consuming)

Bruised leaves of Mallow can be used as a poultice to remove splinters and thorns; even with the threat of Zombies, it is important to treat minor wounds like these so you're performing at your peak. (More in the companion booklet. All in all, it is a very useful plant to source which is quite lucky because it grows practically everywhere.

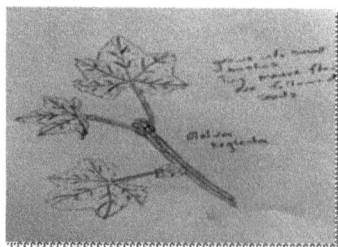

Sticky weed (Cleavers) (Galium aparine)

This annoying plant (annoying because it will cling to your clothes if you brush up against it and the seeds are hard to clean off) could be your saviour in the winter and spring months. All parts of the plant are edible so it is easy to use as you would any green leafy vegetable; dried leaves make a tea with cleansing and detoxing properties. It is very high in Vitamin C, and silica (great to help restore broken nails).

When the seed pods are brown and dried, they can be ground and used as a caffeine free coffee, so if they're stuck on your clothes wait until you get back into the safety of your compound and gather them up as you pick them off your clothes.

The roots of this plant are edible but are also good for dying fabrics if you ever reach the point when you can begin to worry about the colour of your clothing.

Grows: Late winter, Spring

Galium aparine

grows in long strands covering everything that sticky seeds attach. burning fronds.

Goosefoot (Fat Hen) (Chenopodium album)

Related to Spinach, the leaves of Goosefoot can be eaten as a vegetable either cooked or raw but eat it sparingly raw as it contains some oxalic acid (bad in large doses). The seeds are ripe when the leaves start to fall from the plant. They are high in protein, Vitamin A, calcium, phosphorus, and potassium and can be eaten and prepared much like commercially grown Quinoa which is in the same plant family.

Goosefoot quinoa

It may take a bit of experimenting to get the results right with your undoubtedly less sophisticated cooking equipment, but the basic method to preparing seeds of the Goosefoot plant would be to harvest the seeds, pass them through a screen and shake them out to remove the outer husk then soak the remaining part in water to remove a coating called Saponin which are extremely bitter tasting. After this spread the seed out to dry somewhere to reduce the chance of mould forming. Store in an airtight plastic container (See Tips and hints 5).

Cook as you would for Quinoa by covering with water, bringing it to the boil then reducing to a simmer until the water is absorbed. Add some flavouring, vegetables and/or weeds and herbs.

Be careful also if you have hay fever as the pollen of this plant can be an allergen, the last thing you need when foraging for food is an attack of sneezing which is bound to attract Zombies!

All parts of the closely related Good King Henry (Chenopodium bonus-henricus; not a joke name BTW) can be eaten but particularly the reddish coloured seeds can be dried and ground to use as flour which is in some part helpful to the flour accessibility problem.

Grows: Spring and Summer

Ribwort Plantain (Plantago lanceolata)

The leaves of this plant can be eaten as any other green leafy vegetable. The Midrib of the leaf can be tough in older leaves so just cook it for a bit longer or try to remove them with a sharp blade (of which you should have plenty).

The seeds can be dried and ground into flour if can gather enough. It can be added to existing stores of flour to extend it.

**Use sparingly as it is high in oxalic acid that can be dangerous if too much is eaten; although I suppose dying of hunger might be worse?

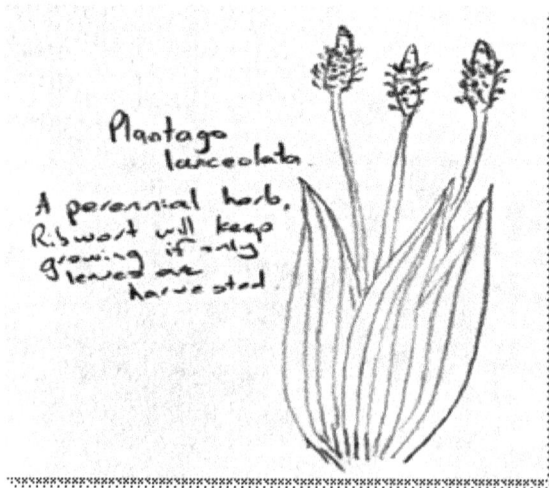

Plantago lanceolata.
A perennial herb, Ribwort will keep growing if only 3 leaves are harvested.

Black Nightshade (Solanum nigra)

Black Nightshade is often mistakenly called Deadly Nightshade. Deadly Nightshade is a different plant, Atropa belladonna. If you eat Atropa belladonna you will just be dead, not undead or best-case scenario, quite ill for a bit which is not very useful for survival. Luckily Deadly Nightshade is not common in Australia so unless you are in another country you should be okay to eat Black Nightshade. If you are in another country just make really sure of what you are eating, maybe just try not to eat anything with 'nightshade' in its name and as always, if you're not sure, just don't eat it.

Black Nightshade is an annual plant that has little white star shaped flowers followed by black berries. The berries are not edible until they are black so don't eat the green ones.

Black nightshade is in the same family as potatoes so the same follows, don't eat the green berries on a potato plant!.

Black Nightshade leaves can be eaten in salads and the black berries can be added into sweets and jams if you're lucky enough to have sweets and jams. As with flour, obtaining enough sugar to make a good jam will be problematic if you haven't got a good supply.

Grows: most of the year

*A note about eating weeds sprayed with herbicide:

Spraying will probably not be a problem in the world after the zombie apocalypse, so you don't really need to wash these plants except to get rid of dirt and possibly animal excrement.

shanprimroseart

Chapter 3: Tips and hints on surviving in a post-zombie apocalypse world

(thoughts and prayers)

Now you have some idea of which plants you would normally have disregarded in your previous life, that will now make up most of your survival diet, we need to take some time to consider a couple of tips and hints that will help to keep your chin up and firmly joined to your head; A depressed person is less likely to be able to fend off a ravenous Zombie!

I've tried some of these recipes, and to be honest they can be pretty awful, so you may need to experiment a little, once you're sure you will be surviving for a little while longer, to try and make them enjoyable. Some of these tips and hints may help.

Tips and hints 1: Add some colour.

While you are foraging for the edible parts of plants that will make up the body of your insubstantial (let's be honest) meal, keep an eye out for edible flowers such as Borage, Violets, Calendula, and Nasturtiums. The bright, cheerful parts of plants that have been designed to attract pollinating insects will add a cheerfulness which may serve to make your dystopian existence that little bit more bearable

Make sure, however, to not take all the flowers as they are required for the plant to reproduce and support you (hopefully) into the future.

Tips and hints 2: Ration, ration, ration

Your old life is over. It has been swept into a past that will never be recovered in your (hopefully a bit longer) lifetime. This means the old ways of using more than we need are no longer sustainable. I am hoping you have found a source of food supplies that will last for some time yet, but this is not a thing that can be guaranteed. This means you need to ration what you have so it lasts.

Case in point: one resource that is particularly relevant to cooking is what you use to season your food to make it palatable i.e. salt and pepper. Salt may be obtained by evaporating sea water, but this is no good If you are inland. Pepper is a spice that comes from mainly tropical parts of the world, so depending on where you are, this may be problematic. I would highly recommend rationing these two long lasting ingredients.

Tips and hints 3: Grow garlic

We have discussed the need to season your food and with luck you have a store of salt and hopefully pepper too. The other seasoning for food that is both widely available and easy to grow is garlic.

If you find a whole clove of garlic in your foraging, don't be tempted to eat all of it at once, smaller cloves that are peeled off the larger clove can be placed into soil and will grow into more garlic (it can take a long time, but it will be worth the effort if you are still alive)

Tips and hints 4: Find Chickens

Try to find an abandoned flock of chickens. Eggs and the occasional chicken (Protein!) will be a highly regarded addition to your normal diet. This is obviously problematic in some locations, especially cities, as most people in cities did not have chickens. Don't be discouraged, the movement toward slow foods in our past world was resulting in chickens and even bees becoming more common in urban areas, so it's not impossible!

Chickens may be challenging to have living in close proximity to your compound as they can be quite noisy; noise, as you know, attracts Zombies. The solution may be to keep your flock of chickens in a location that is easily and safely accessible, but at a safe distance. Once again, don't forget you are living in a dog eat dog world, so be on the lookout for marauding groups of 'others' (people who, like you, are just trying to survive but might not be a nice as you)

Tips and hints 5: Collect as many plastic containers with the correct lids as you can.

Storing food properly and safe from insect/rodent attack has never been more important. The old-fashioned Tupperware container is probably best so I would look in kitchen cupboards first, the war on plastic may have had unwanted side effects if solid, long lasting plastic aren't available; Tupperware is king.

Tips and hints 6: Test first!

I should probably have put this one as the very first tip. I'm hoping you haven't tried some of these plants out and suffered from an allergic reaction! Before you do try anything for the very first time, it is a good idea to try a very small piece and wait to see if there is any reaction other than a "Yum! That's really good!". Look for my companion book on medicinal weeds: Surviving the Zombie Apocalypse: A Quick guide to fixing simple Ailments. (Note: This guide is intended only for minor ailments such as scrapes and burns. It will not, I repeat NOT help with the loss of limbs, Zombie Viruses, or other life-threatening injuries/disease.)

Tips and Hints 7: Harvesting tip

Unless you are harvesting the roots of these plants you can cut the leaves off close to the base and leave the stem to regrow; Dandelions, Thistles, and Portulaca in particular, will do this. As I have mentioned before, make sure to leave enough flowers and rooting tubers etc (as applicable) to allow for sustainable harvesting through into the future.

Tips and hints 8: Onion weed! (Allium triquetrum)

Yes, Onion weed is edible. You know what onion weed is, it is that extremely testing weed with the pretty white flower you always wish was a snowdrop. You can eat all parts of it. If you have had no luck with sourcing garlic, this weed can be used instead, the leaves and flowers have an oniony taste while the bulb is mildly 'garlicy'. At last, you have found a use for this pesky weed; pity it's taken a zombie apocalypse.

Tips and hints 9: Duct tape

Find as much duct tape as you can and guard it with your life!

A few final words.

I mentioned water in the very first paragraph of this book, but I can't stress enough how important it will be to ensure this resource remains easy to access, and permanently free from contaminants; don't let the zombies near it!

So, there you have it. I am hopeful this booklet contains at least one or two helpful pieces of information to help you survive the end of our civilisation as we know it, it could mean the difference between the survival of the human race and extinction.

No pressure.

The final words of advice I have are these:

Aim for the head! It's the only way to kill them!

-//-

The End

Links: If you want a bit more information and you're not in any danger of either losing your internet connection or of being attacked by zombies, take the time to look at these pages. My best advice is to learn a bit about what you can eat before you actually need to.

https://www.eatweeds.co.uk/dandelion-root-coffee-recipe

https://www.thekitchn.com/fresh-summer-recipe-dandelion-pumpkin-seed-pesto-173211

https://www.allrecipes.com/recipe/214172/fried-dandelions-appalachian-style/

https://www.gardenguides.com/95948-cook-fresh-dandelion-root.html

gardenbetty.com

https://wildfoodgirl.com/

http://persephonemagazine.com/2012/10/eating-the-weeds-goosefoot/

footnote: At the time of finalising this book we have been living through the Corona Virus Pandemic. The first thing people began to hoard was toilet paper. Take note of that and prepare!

Frances Bryant, 2020.

Book Two

Unexpectedly Edible

Common plants
you could eat
(If you had to...)

Frances Bryant

Unexpectedly
Edible:
Common plants you could eat.
(If you had to)

Frances Bryant.

For Rosemary.

Friend, client, mentor.

Plant list

- Pine Trees (Pinus sp.)
- Water lilies (Nymphaea sp.)
- Dahlia (Dahlia sp.)
- Begonia (Begonia x tuberhybridia, B. semperflorens)
- Aloe Vera
- Oak (Quercus sp)
- Canna lily (Canna indica)
- Day lily (Hemerocallis fulva)
- Tree ferns (Cyathea sp., Dicksonia sp.)
- Chinese Toon (Cedrela sinensis)
- Callistemon sp.
- Fuchsia berries

Chapters

-Introduction

-Plants

-A few final words

-References

(Further reading including links to online sources
used in research)

-/-

Introduction

The food we eat in western countries is generally supplied to us from supermarkets, restaurants, and sometimes even fast-food joints. Some of us are lucky enough to live with patches of earth where we can choose to grow plants commonly known to be edible. These plants can be supplied to us as seeds or seedlings grown by organisations that have chosen their products by availability and consumer demand i.e., seasonal plants that have sold well in the past.

We become accustomed to eating the foods we are most familiar with. This can vary from community to community, but those communities are also eating foods they are in the habit of eating. For instance, one community might usually have Bok Choy as a green vegetable while another may be more familiar with Broccoli as a green vegetable, although this is in no way set in stone. We who live in western countries are lucky to have a variety of foods from different food cultures available to us.

While we have become comfortable eating certain plants, there are many, many other varieties of plants that for one reason or another have not become mainstays of our diets; they have fallen out of favour or simply not been used enough in the culinary arts to have become popular, or even to be recognisable anymore as being edible.

This book is an introduction to, and perhaps an awakening to, plants that are commonly available, or near enough to commonly available, or growing in our gardens that may be eaten if you needed to or wanted to; the unexpectedly edible.

This book is in no way a definitive guide to changing the way you eat, including these plants in your daily diet forever, it is merely to give you an idea of which plants you are growing for ornamental purposes, but you could also eat.

I can't imagine a situation whereby these foods would be all you would have to eat, that would be a dire situation indeed!

Enjoy this peek into the unexpectedly edible and hope you never need this information for your very survival.

Frances Bryant.

Unexpectedly Edible Plants:

Pinus sp.

The humble Pine Tree, a tree commonly used as decoration to celebrate Christmas in many western countries. A tree that is also considered to be weedy in some parts of the world. This tree (and others included in Pinus sp.) has many parts that can be consumed by humans.

Bark

Tree trunks are covered in a protective layer of bark. Underneath the first layer of bark there is a layer called the Cambium layer. This is the part of the bark that is edible.

The Cambium layer is the matter used by the tree to transport water and nutrients up and down the trunk of the tree and out into its extremities.

If you are harvesting the Cambium layer for eating, care must be taken not to remove too much from an individual tree. If the Cambium layer is damaged too extensively the tree can become too damaged, or infected, and can die.

Luckily, Pine trees often have quite large trunks so parts can be removed from separate areas, thus reducing these risks.

The method for removal of the Cambium layer is to use a sharp knife or small axe and cut down through the outer bark layer, down through the Cambium layer until you reach the next layer underneath which is the growth from previous years.

Once you have carved down into the bark, continue cutting to create a rectangular shape no wider than 5cm, gently use the knife or small axe to slice off the bark, complete with the cambium layer making sure not to cut into the next layer underneath. When you have removed the piece of bark, complete with the edible piece of cambium layer, gently slice the cambium layer off and it is ready to prepare for eating.

Cooking

Eating it raw is possible, but not advised; the best ways to cook it are to either boil or fry.

As with most foods, boiling can reduce the nutrition value, but it will completely palatable. Adding other vegetables and garlic for flavour will create a lovely soup or even a stew.

Frying the bark is the best option. Strip the bark into very thin strips and fry with butter or oil, seasoning with salt and pepper.

Another valuable method of using pine park is to dry it out completely, either in an oven or air dried, then grind it into a fine powder which can be used as flour!

(If you have read my book 'Food for Survivors of the Zombie Apocalypse: An introduction to foraging for Edible Weeds' (link in the reference section) you will know one of the main issues I discovered for surviving on foraged food was the lack of flour to use in making other edible weeds palatable. This is a possible solution!)

Pine Needles

Pine needles make a nutritious, healthy, and tasty tea.

Method:

Gather a handful of leaves without any other pieces such as twigs or bits of cone.

Chop them finely, place in a pot and cover with boiling water. Let it steep for a few minutes until it is the colour of green tea, strain, and enjoy.

Pine Pollen

The pollen can only be collected at certain times of the year. Pine trees generally have an extremely large amount of pollen, and it is carried all over the tree so taking a small amount will not affect its fertility.

The pollen is carried on the male cones, and you will be able to see yellowish powder.

Shake this powder into a container which can take a while but is easily done.

Use the pollen as a thickener, a flour substitute (another one!), and for coating foods before cooking or frying.

Pine Nuts

Pine nuts are very commonly used in 'normal' cookery. Pine nuts can be gathered and used as per normal. They are also very high in nutrients if picked freshly.

Not all Pine species have seeds that are large enough to be useful but if enough of the smaller species are gathered, they can be used in any way you would normally use Pine Nuts.

*** Note ***

Please note that there are many **Pine-like** trees that are edible, but there are a few that **definitely are not** such as the

-Norfolk Island Pine (Araucaria heterophylla),

- the Yew (Taxus)

- and Ponderosa Pines (Pinus ponderosa — aka Western Yellow Pine, Blackjack Pine, or Bull Pine).

Please make sure you know what you are eating!

If you are not sure, do not eat it!

-/-

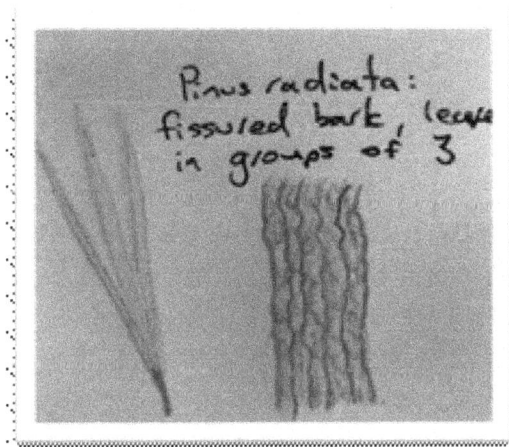

Pinus radiata: fissured bark, leave in groups of 3

Waterlilies

Nymphaea sp

The Waterlily has been used as an ornamental plant in ponds and waterways for centuries. In Egyptian, Hindu, and Buddhist culture the Waterlily represented both the sun and rebirth; the flower opens in the morning and closes at night.

As well as being a useful ornamental plant, many parts of the Waterlily are edible. The new leaves, tubers, flowers, and even seeds can all be eaten.

Leaves

Picking new leaves ensures they are tender as they can become tough and bitter as they grow. They can be steamed or boiled and added to soups or stews, or if they are young and tender, chopped finely and added to salads.

Flowers

Pick the unopened buds of the waterlily (if you can bear losing the gorgeous flowers). These can be eaten raw in a salad or coated in seasoned flour and fried.

Tubers

Some species of Waterlily have smaller, less palatable tubers. Two of the best waterlily species for eating tubers are N. *tuberosa* and N. *alba*. There is some slight toxicity in some of the other species' tubers so if you're unsure which species you have, either eat only a small part or avoid altogether. **As always, only eat something if you know what it is.**

If you do have one of the species mentioned and you do decide to try the tuber, it can be eaten as you would a potato or any other starchy, tuberous vegetable.

The tubers are generally best for eating before flowering.

Seeds

After flowering, small pods are formed which contain seeds. These seeds can be harvested and either popped like popcorn or boiled, dried, and ground into a powder which can be used as flour (I don't know what I was worried about!)

Dahlia sp

Another highly ornamental flowering plant, the Dahlia, has a 'tuber' (not technically a tuber) that was sometimes eaten as a vegetable by the peoples of Central America.

The Dahlias we see flowering in our herbaceous borders in late summer and autumn has been hybridised quite a lot over the centuries since it was introduced to western culture as an ornamental flower. The main species seen in cultivation today are D. x *pinnata* and D. *coccinea*. The flowers have been the focus of breeders over the centuries, but with this breeding intervention the qualities of the tubers have changed as well.

Some Dahlias have large, fleshy tubers while other have smaller, tougher tubers. The larger the tuber, the more likely it is to be softer and more palatable so use these ones; they can be used as you would use a potato or any other tuberous vegetable although it is generally best to peel the skin off as it can be tough and bitter.

Flowers

Dahlia flowers can be picked at any stage and added to salads for a bit of colour.

A Dahlia tuber recently harvested, then washed and cut.

Notice the thick skin on the cut tuber on the right.

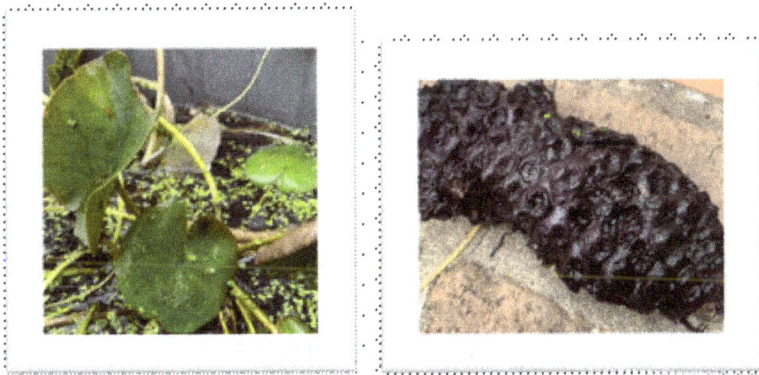

The Water lily 'Tuber' is of a much rougher texture.

Washed and peeled, it is prepared in a similar manner to the Dahlia.

Water lily leaves can be eaten fresh, steamed, boiled, and fried

Begonia

(Begonia x *tuberhybrida*, B. *semperflorens*)

There are many different types of Begonias with varying types of growth habit, but they have similar flowers and leaf textures, albeit with a few varying, highly ornamental shapes. Begonia species have been used in the past by many different cultures as food and for some medicinal applications, but I will focus on two very commonly grown Begonias.

Because B. x *tuberhybrida* (Tuberous Begonia) and B. *semperflorens* (Bedding or Wax begonia) are very commonly grown, I will say these are the plants I mean when discussing edible Begonias.

The flowers, leaves, and stems of these two Begonia species are edible.

Flowers

With all flowers, unless they are growing inside, in more stable conditions, pick them early in the morning when they are at their best. Begonia flowers have a crunchy texture and slightly sour taste. Their bright colours are a great addition to any salad or even as decoration on a cake. They can also be pureed and added to dips and sauces.

Leaves

The leaves of Begonia are quite fleshy and interestingly, grow in the same direction the flowers are facing. The leaves are best eaten cooked, boiled or steamed; they can be added to other green vegetables and deep frying them in hot oil will make them into 'chips'.

Stems

Larger stems can be used as you would use Rhubarb.

NOTE

All parts of Begonia sp. Contain Oxalic acid which can be toxic at high levels, so it is suggested to not eat them in large quantities, or too often.

Begonia Spread:

Blend the following ingredients together to make a tasty spread or dip:

- 225g Cream Cheese
- ¼ cup strawberry or Raspberry Jam
- Fruit juice or water to soften
- 1/3 cup pureed Begonia petals

Begonia Tartlet:

You will need

- 85g Cream Cheese

- ¼ tsp sugar

- precooked tartlet cases

- two cups Begonia leaves

- Blend the cream cheese and sugar together

-1/2 cup water

-Place Begonia leaves in a pot, add the water and bring to the boil. Cook until they are reduced to a paste.

- add the Begonia leaves to the cream cheese and sugar mixture

- put the leaf and cheese mixture into the tartlet cases

- Bake 30mins in a low oven (140C)

*recipe taken from: www.eattheweeds.com

Aloe Vera

Most of us are familiar with Aloe vera. This unassuming succulent sits in our gardens waiting for when we get bitten or have a small cut, which is when we break a stem open to get at the soothing, healing, gelatinous interior to slather on top. This isn't the one you eat.

Aloe *vera var. chinensis* is the one most usually grown in our gardens and not considered edible, but there is another one that is available both to grow and to buy in some specialty supermarkets, Aloe vera *barbadensis var. miller. This one is edible.*

The difference between the two plants is quite distinct, the medicinal Aloe (*chinensis*) is smaller, a pale green, with pale speckles. The other, edible Aloe (*barbadensis var. miller) is much larger, a darker green, and has no speckles on its older growth.*

Once you have determined if your Aloe vera is of the edible variety, or if you have bought is specifically from a specialty supermarket, it can be sliced and used.

NOTE

Aloe vera is not suitable for some people. If you notice any symptoms after eating, please discontinue its use.

To use the Aloe:

- Cut the stem into small (2 or 3 inch) segments.
- Slice the top layer of each segment off and scrape out the gelatinous innards. These can be kept for use in a smoothie or even as a cooling lotion for your skin.
- If you are eating the Aloe raw, soak it in water for 10 minutes to soften it.
- Use the Aloe in salads or chop up further and use as a garnish or in things such as salsas and soups.
- Dip raw Aloe into hummus or any other dip.

Aloe Salsa

Mix equal amounts of chopped Aloe and tomatoes.

Season with salt and pepper.

Add chopped Coriander or parsley.

If you want a chunky salsa leave it as it is or put it through a blender to make a paste for a dip.

Add chilli for a spicier blend.

*Recipe taken from www.wikihow.com/Eat-Aloe-Vera

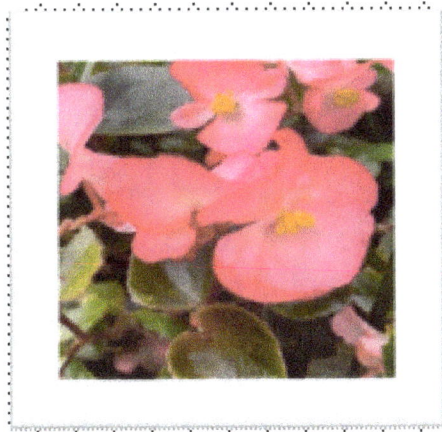

Bedding Begonias (B. semperflorens) is a common plant for gardens and indoor growing. The flowers are edible.

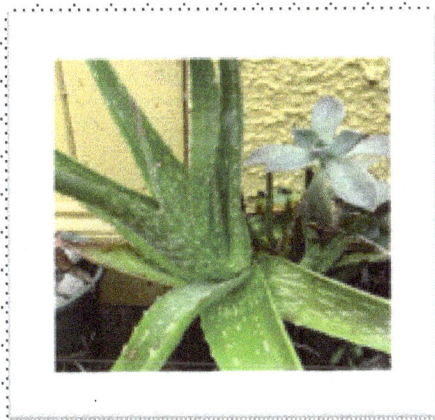

This is the medicinal Aloe vera (A. vera var. sinensis). The edible Aloe can sometimes be found in specialty Asian stores. Know what you are eating!

Oak Trees

Quercus sp.

The majestic Oak tree has been a part of northern hemisphere civilisations for centuries. The large tree is very long-lived and has been revered as being sacred by some societies.

There are many, many species of Oak. They have a variety of sizes and leaf shapes, but they all bear their fruit as acorns which have an extremely hard outer shell.

The leaves and bark of Oak trees can be used to make a tea by steeping a handful of each in boiling water, straining then drinking, but the main source of food from the tree is this acorn. See the section on Pine species for directions on how to cut the bark.

As I have said, acorns have an extremely hard outer shell and are most usually packed full of toxic tannins which, if not released from the acorn, can cause Kidney damage with prolonged use.

Don't be turned off by this though as the process of 'leaching' (see below) releases this toxin, making the acorns palatable for humans.

Once the process of leaching has been carried out, dry the acorns, grind them up and use them as flour (Again! I don't know what I was worried about!).

Leaching:

There are two ways of leaching the tannins out of the acorns: Cold leaching and hot leaching. Each method leaves the acorns suitable for different uses: cold for grinding and making flour, hot for roasting for snacks and coffee.

*I have provided a link for a web page that goes into the detail, as the process is longer than what this book provides for: britishlocalfood.com/leaching-acorns

Once you have successfully leached the toxic tannins out of the acorns they can be used for flour, roasted snacks, and coffee. The flour produced has the added benefit to some of being Gluten Free.

Acorn Pancakes:

1 cup acorn flour

1 cup white flour

1 tsp sugar

2tsp baking powder

2 eggs

¼ cup butter (melted)

1 cup milk

Mix flours, sugar, and baking powder in a bowl.

Mix lightly together eggs, butter, and milk.

Combine adding a little more milk if it needs it.

Heat a fry pan, add butter then pancake batter at whichever size suits.

Cook one side until bubbles appear and burst, flip over to finish cooking ad remove from the pan. Put on a plate, drizzle over with Maple syrup or whichever topping you prefer.

*Recipe taken from britishlocalfood.com

-/-

Canna Lily

Canna *indica* (Canna *edulis*)

The Canna Lily is not actually a Lily. They are a rhizomatous perennial, and not a bulb, as most lilies are. Originally a tropical plant, may cultivars have been bred to live happily in temperate climates.

The bright, tropical looking flowers can be eaten raw in salads etc and can also be chopped finely and added to dips. The rhizome from which the long, fleshy stalks rise is also edible.

Cultivars that have longer rhizomes are less fibrous and as such are more palatable but peeling and grating before boiling the rhizome makes it even softer still; add finely chopped Rhizomes to a slow cooked stew. Baking the rhizomes after peeling is also an option.

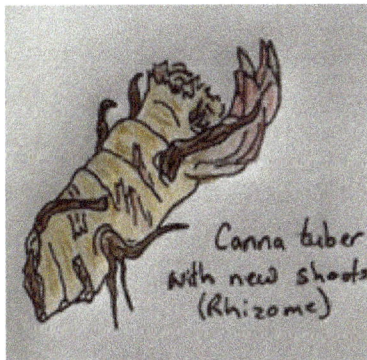

Canna tuber with new shoots (Rhizome)

-/-

Daylilies

(Hemerocallis sp.)

What a beautiful plant. Daylilies are a favourite in the garden over many parts of the world. As with Canna Lilies, they are not lilies either but a tuberous perennial.

The Daylily has been commonly eaten in some Asian countries for centuries, but this fact has become lost in western cultures as they have become a popular ornamental garden plant.

All parts of the plant are edible: unopened buds, flowers, stalks, shoots, and roots. Just be aware that Daylilies live up to their name and their flowers do, indeed, only last one day, so plan ahead if you want to use opened flowers in any recipe.

Unopened buds:

Pick the buds as they form to be used as you would use beans or peas or coat them in batter and deep fry.

Flowers:

Once the flowers have opened, they can be eaten as many other flowers can be eaten. Throw them on top of a salad, as decorations on cakes etc, or chopped and added to sauces and dips for colour. When dried, they can be used as a thickener for soups and stews.

New shoots:

as the new shoots appear from the roots (tubers) they can be harvested and stir fried with a bit of garlic as a green vegetable.

Stalks:

Cut the stems just above the roots and boil or steam before adding them to greens or into other dishes as a vegetable.

Roots:

The thick, tuberous roots of the daylily can be roasted or boiled and used as any starchy root vegetable.

Use the new growth coming from the centre of the Daylily plant for maximum tenderness.

Fishbone (Boston, Sword) Fern

(Nephrolepis *cordifolia*)

We have all more than likely had this fern in our garden at some point. It is the kind of plant that sits there for a while doing nothing, so you think you can just leave it alone. The one day you look back in that slightly damp, shady area and it has taken over. You rip it all out and have piles of green fronds and roots along with quite a few round, tuber-like balls. Well, you can eat these round, tuber-like balls.

After being washed, these 'tubers', or water storage units, can be eaten raw, chopped, grated into salads, or roasted and added to other vegetables. They are usually quite small so their roasting time will be quite short.

There are other ground growing ferns with edible parts but as this book is focused on commonly gown plants, I won't include them. Foragers will identify ferns that are palatable for humans, but as some are known to have small carcinogenic properties, it is best to leave that to the experts and have expert tuition on their preparations:

survivalfreedom.com/how-to-identify-and-eat-edible.ferns/

-/-

Chinese Toon

(Cedrela *sinensis*)

This tree will grow nicely green over the summer then drop all its leaves in Autumn. When the temperature rises and the days start getting longer, new shoots will appear, and they will be a beautifully vivid pink colour.

Those beautiful pink leaves have a deliciously crunchy feel and an oniony taste. They are used in some Chinese cooking but are not often eaten in western diets.

Pick the fresh young leaves, chop them finely and use them either raw or cooked in any dish you need an oniony/garlicky flavour.

Toona Fried Egg:

A handful of fresh, new Toona leaves

2 eggs

Blanch the toona leaves until they are soft (they may change to green but will retain the garlicky flavour),

Beat the two eggs until combined,

Add the leaves to the egg and stir until mixed,

Place egg mix into a frypan and leave to cook through,

Turn and finish cooking on the other side, then serve.

Toona Fritters:

2 cups plain flour

2 tsp baking powder

2 eggs lightly beaten.

¼ tsp salt

1 cup chopped and blanched Toona leaves.

Sift the dry ingredients together,

Make a well in the centre and put in the two eggs,

Fold all together,

Add the blanched Toona leaves and keep folding it all together until well blended,

place tablespoons of the fritter mix into a hot frypan with some oil,

Fry on one side until cooked through then turn over and finish cooking on the other side,

Serve hot.

-/-

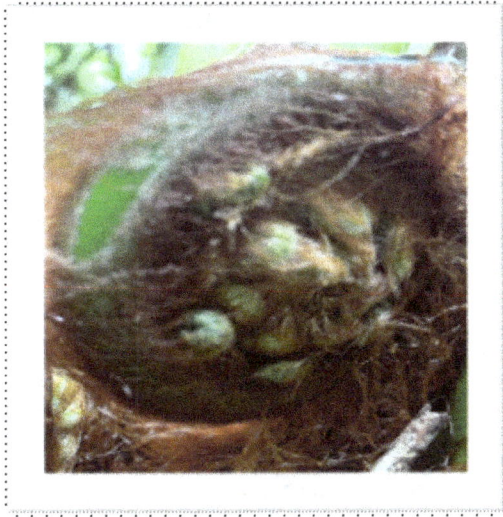

This is the new growth of a tree fern. Curled up un the centre of the older fronds at the top of the trunk.

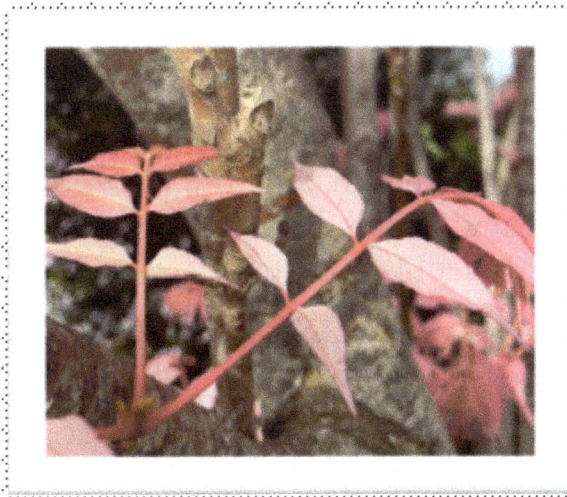

New growth of Cedrela sinensis

Tree Ferns

(Dicksonia sp., Cyathea sp.)

In the temperate rainforests of Australia and New Zealand (and some other regions), Tree Ferns grow quite easily and prolifically, they are also a lovely addition to any home garden. If there was some kind of food emergency, you could also eat parts of it.

The new leaf growth comes from the centre of the trunk at the top of the trunk. These are more tender than older parts and as such can be steamed or boiled and used as a vegetable, or even roasted.

The inner part of the trunk can also be eaten but this involves cutting the Tree Fern down and removing the centre of the stump. This whitish, pulpy matter can be baked or even eaten raw.

The bonus of having to cut the Tree Fern down is you can replant the trunk making the plant lower down, thus making the new fronds (which as you recall grow from the top of the trunk) easier to harvest.

There is information to suggest that Tree ferns do contain carcinogens that can build up in your body, however, so eating them too often (or at all) could be considered unwise.

-/-

Bottlebrush, Ti Tree, Melaleuca

(Callistemon sp., Leptospermum sp.,Melaleuca sp.)

Writing this book in Australia, I cannot go past mentioning a few Australian natives.

The main use for these highly ornamental shrubs is making tea from their leaves. Some species are better for this use than others, for example C. *citrinus* has a lemony flavour as indicated in the name.

The usual method of tea making is whereby a handful of leaves is lightly chopped and steeped in boiling water then strained and drunk.

Another way of making a sweet tea is to pick flowers and steep these in boiling water to make use of the sweetness of the nectar. Some of these species are widely used as a source of nectar for honeybees.

There is a large amount of information available regarding the use of Australian native plants as food. I feel this information is best disseminated by the original people who used these foods to survive over centuries, so I won't go into it here. I'm sure there are many Australian native plants used as ornaments in our gardens that would be unexpectedly edible!

-/-

Fuchsia sp.

This gorgeous shrub with its ballerina flowers was the plant that sparked my interest in which common garden plants that can be eaten, leading to this book.

While I have found little information on other parts of the fuchsia plant which may be edible, I do know the 'fruit' which is left when the flower has finished is indeed something you can eat.

The many cultivars of this immensely popular plant have different levels of 'berriness" (made up word) with some being small and red, and others being large and a dark purple/black colour. They are all edible but have a different taste and/or texture. The sweeter ones remind me a little of Kiwifruit.

The slightly sweet 'fruit' of the Fuchsia can be added to a fruit salad, used in muffins, made into jams, or just eaten as a gardener's snack.

Use the berries soon after picking as they do not last long.

A few final words

This brings me to the end of the book.

I hope you have read something in here that has piqued an interest in looking at your garden in a different light.

While you might not necessarily be interested in trying out anything you have discovered, you now have an increased knowledge that may do you some good in the future. The most important thing I cannot stress enough is to know exactly what you are eating; if in doubt, leave it out.

In full disclosure, I haven't tried these plants except the Chinese Toon and the Fuchsia Berries, both of which I find surprisingly tasty. Who knows? In the future I just might, I hope you do too!

Frances Bryant

2021.

References

Research for this book has mainly been done via online sources. The sources for recipes in the book have been noted alongside whilst below is a list of other sources used.

I have also included a link to my first book: Food for survivors of the Zombie Apocalypse: An introduction to Edible Weeds.

There are many, many sites on the internet with a huge amount of information regarding edible plants, these are just the tip of the iceberg.

https://laidbackgardener.blog/tag/begonias-are-edible/

https://hub.suttons.co.uk/blog/general/edible-tuberous-begonias

https://www.skilledsurvival.com/products

www.survivaliq.com/survival/edible-and-medicinal-plants-water-lily.htm great source of info on lots of plants.

https://www.skilledsurvival.com/eating-pine-how-to-eat-a-pine-tree/#:~:text=%20Edible%20Parts%20of%20The%20Pine%20Tree%20,an%20excellent%20survival%20edible.%20It%20tastes...%20More%20

Food For Survivors of the Zombie Apocalypse: An introduction to foraging for edible 'weeds'. eBook: Shingles-Bryant, Frances , Primrose, Shan: Amazon.com.au: Books

-/-

Final, final word

As we know there are plants we can eat, and you have been warned (repeatedly) not to eat anything if you're not completely sure what it is, I feel it's important to point out there are plants you simply MUST NOT eat. Here are some:

Daffodils, Narcissus sp.

Castor Oil Plant, Ricinus communis

Oleander, Nerium Oleander

Deadly Nightshade, Atropa belladonna (not to be confused with Black Nightshade, Solanum nigra)

White Cedar Tree, Melia azedarach

Angel's Trumpet, Brugmansia sp.

Arum Lily, Zantedeschia aethiopica

Belladonna Lily, Amaryllis belladonna

Daphne, Daphne sp.

Japanese Windflower, Anenome hupehensis

Lantana, Lantana camara

There are plenty more, so be careful out there! FB.

Conclusion

Well, there you have it. With these little bits of info you should be able to manage surviving a survivable crisis. In the event of a nulcear winter, it would be much more difficult, but then, would it be worth surviving that if you couldn't ever have a great meal again?

The most important thing anybody should take out of books regarding food you wouldn't normally eat is to be very careful. Do NOT eat anything if you're not 100% certain it is edible.

If you've never tried it before, test a tiny bit first to see if there are any physical effects such as tingling lips or your throat closing over causing you to stop breathing.

If you're not sure, don't eat it!

Frances Bryant

2024.

Left blank for notes

www.ingramcontent.com/pod-product-compliance
Lightning Source LLC
Chambersburg PA
CBHW080926050426
42334CB00055B/2815